The Unshakable TRUTH® Journey

GROWTH GUIDES
for Adults

Accepted

Experience God's Unconditional Love

JOSH McDOWELL
SEAN McDOWELL

HARVEST HOUSE PUBLISHERS

EUGENE, OREGON

Cover by Koechel Peterson & Associates, Inc., Minneapolis, Minnesota

ACCEPTED—EXPERIENCE GOD'S UNCONDITIONAL LOVE
Course 4 of The Unshakable Truth® Journey Growth Guides
Copyright © 2011 by Josh McDowell Ministry and Sean McDowell
Published by Harvest House Publishers
Eugene, Oregon 97402
www.harvesthousepublishers.com

ISBN 978-0-7369-4644-5

Printed in the United States of America

11 12 13 14 15 16 17 18 19 / VP-SK / 10 9 8 7 6 5 4 3 2 1

CONTENTS

About the Authors

Authors Josh and Sean McDowell collaborated with their writer to bring you this Unshakable Truth Journey course. The content is based upon Scripture and the McDowells' book *The Unshakable Truth.*®

Over 45-plus years, **Josh McDowell** has spoken to more than 10 million people in 120 countries about the evidence for Christianity and the difference the Christian faith makes in the world. He has authored or coauthored more than 120 books (with more than 51 million copies in print), including such classics as *More Than a Carpenter* and *New Evidence That Demands a Verdict*.

Sean McDowell is an educator and a popular speaker at schools, churches, and conferences nationwide. He is author of *Ethix: Being Bold in a Whatever World*, coauthor of *Understanding Intelligent Design*, and general editor of *Apologetics for a New Generation* and *The Apologetics Study Bible for Students*. He is currently pursuing a PhD in apologetics and worldview studies. Sean's website, www.seanmcdowell.org, offers his blog, many articles and videos, and much additional curriculum.

About the Writer

Dave Bellis is a ministry consultant focusing on ministry planning and product development. He is a writer, producer, and product developer. He and his wife, Becky, have two grown children and live in northeastern Ohio.

Acknowledgments

We would like to thank the many people who brought creativity and insight to forming this course:

Terri Snead and David Ferguson of Great Commandment Network for their writing insights for the TruthTalk and Truth Encounter sections of this study guide.

Terry Glaspey for his insights and guidance as he helped in the development of the Unshakable Truth Journey concept.

Paul Gossard for his skillful editing of this manuscript.

And finally, the entire team at Harvest House, who graciously endured the process with us.

Josh McDowell
Sean McDowell
Dave Bellis

What Is the Unshakable Truth Journey All About?

Y ou hear people talk about having a personal relationship with God and knowing Christ. But what does that really mean? Sure, they probably are saying they are a Christian and God has personally forgiven them of their sins. But is that all of what being a Christian really is—being a person forgiven by God?

We are here to say that being a follower of Christ is much, much more than that. Everything you are and what you are becoming as a person is wrapped up in it. When Jesus said he was "the way, the truth, and the life" (John 14:6) he was offering us a supernatural way to follow in his way, his truth, and his life. As we do, we begin to understand what we were meant to know and be and how we were meant to live. Actually, when we become a follower of Christ we begin to take on Jesus' view of the world and begin to think like and be motivated like and live like Christ. And that brings incredible joy and satisfaction to life.

So when we see life and relationships as Jesus sees them, we begin to get a clear picture of who we are and discover our true identity. We begin to realize why we are here and recognize our purpose and meaning in life. We begin to know where we are going and experience our destiny and mission in a life larger than ourselves. Being a Christian—a committed follower of Christ—unlocks our identity, purpose, and destiny in life. It is then that the natural process of spiritual reproduction takes place. That is when imparting the faith to our family and others around us becomes a reality. But what is involved in being that kind of a follower of Christ—a person who has joy and satisfaction in life and knows how to effectively impart the faith to the next generation?

The Unshakable Truth Journey gets to the core of what being a true follower of Christ means and what knowing Christ is all about. Together you and your group will begin a journey that will last a lifetime. It is a journey into what you as a follower of Christ are to believe biblically, how you process your beliefs into core values, and how you live them out in all your relationships. In fact, we will take the core truths of Christianity and break them down into a five-step process:

1. ***What truths do you as a Christian believe biblically?***

    In the first step you and your group will interact
    with what we as Christians believe about God,
    his Word, and so on.

2. ***Why do you believe those truths?***

    Sure, you can say you believe certain truths
    because they are biblical, but when you know
    why they are true it grounds you in your faith.
    Additionally, it gives you confidence to pass
    them on to others—especially your family.

3. ***How are these truths relevant to life?***

    In many respects truth isn't very meaningful
    until you see how it is relevant to your own life.

4. ***How do you live these truths out personally?***

    Knowing how the truth of Christianity is relevant
    is necessary, but what it leads to is understand-
    ing how that truth is to become a living reality in
    your own life. That's where the rubber meets the
    road, so to speak.

5. ***How do you, as a group, live these truths out before
    your community and world?***

    As Christians we are all to be "salt" and "light" to

the world around us. In this step you and your group will discover how to impact your own community with truth that is lived out corporately—as a body.

Be warned! The Unshakable Truth Journey isn't a program to study what Christianity is all about. Simply discovering what something is about has great limitations and ends up being of little value. Rather, this journey is about experiencing firsthand how God's truth is to be experienced in your life right now and, in fact, for the rest of your life. It's is about knowing God's truth in a real, experiential way. The apostle John said, "It is by our actions that we know we are living in the truth" (1 John 3:19). You will be challenged repeatedly to increasingly know certain truths by experiencing them continually in your relationship with God and with those around you. It is then you will be able to pass on this ever-increasing faith journey to your family and friends.

There will be two specific exercises that appear throughout these courses. The first is entitled "Truth Encounter." This section is an invitation for you to stop and carefully reflect on the truth of each session. You'll be asked to encounter a truth of God as you relate personally with Jesus, as you live out the truth of God's Word with your small group, or as you relate personally with his people. Please don't rush past these Truth Encounters. They are designed to equip you in how to experience truth right in the room you're in!

The second exercise is an assignment for the week, called "TruthTalk." The TruthTalks are designed as conversation starters—ways to engage others in spiritual discussions. They will create opportunities for you to share what you've experienced in this course with others around you. This will help you communicate God's truth with others as you share vulnerably about your own Unshakable Truth Journey.

What you discover here is to last a lifetime and beyond because God's truths are designed to be enjoyed forever. You see, experiencing God's truth and knowing him will grow throughout eternity, and your love of him will expand to contain it. And that process begins in the here and now. Your relationship with God may have begun 5 months, 5 years, or 50 years ago—it doesn't matter. The truths explored in these courses are to be applied at every level of life. And what is so encouraging is that while these truths are eternally deep they can be embraced and experienced by even a young child. That is the beauty and mystery of God's truth!

This particular Unshakable Truth Journey is one of 12 different growth guides. All the growth guides are based upon Josh and Sean McDowell's book *The Unshakable Truth*, which is the companion book to this course. The book covers 12 core truths of the Christian faith. The growth guide you have in your hand covers the truth about God's redemption plan. God became human, and his unconditional acceptance defines our worth.

Together we will explore the value he places on us in spite of our sin. These five sessions lay the foundation for how to gain a high sense of worth. Check out the other Unshakable Truth Journey courses in the appendix of this growth guide.

Okay then, let our journey begin.

WHAT WE BELIEVE ABOUT GOD BECOMING HUMAN

As a child growing up, did you experience some kind of rejection or embarrassment from peers or adults? Maybe you were not picked to play on a team, or maybe you were made fun of for being too big, too small, or simply not quite fitting in. We have all felt rejected or embarrassed at some time or another. Describe your experience and how it made you feel.

_____

_____

_____

_____

_____

_____

_____

Our experiences of embarrassment and rejection may often have been cruel and unfair. But some actions deserve rejection. Identify a person currently alive or from history who deserved personal and societal rejection. This would be someone who committed heinous crimes deserving of total rejection, banishment, or even death. Name the person and what he or she did to deserve such harsh judgment.

_____

_____

_____

_____

Now imagine that the heinous crime was committed against you or your family. This person then is your worst enemy. You hate with a passion what they have done. So now imagine yourself walking into the offender's guarded prison cell, wrapping your arms around them, and saying, "I love and accept you for who you are." In your present state of mind and emotions would you find that hard to do? Why or why not?

_____

_____

_____

_____

_____

_____

OUR GROUP OBJECTIVE

To better grasp the meaning of God's unconditional acceptance through the miracle of the incarnation— God's Son taking on human form.

Someone read Romans 5:12 and Ephesians 2:1-3.

As far as a holy and just God is concerned you are guilty of sin and the death sentence has already been handed down. So in God's eyes, how is your guilt and death sentence any different than the dreadful criminal that is your worst enemy? Discuss.

_____

_____

_____

_____

How does God respond to you personally as a guilty sinner? How does he respond to the worst criminal of heinous acts? Someone read Romans 5:6-8, Ephesians 2:3-4, and Hebrews 2:14-15.

Instead of rendering an immediate judgment that you are deserving of eternal death, what did God do?

_____

_____

_____

_____

God Makes His Move First

Contemplate this question for a moment: How is it that God, who is holy, reaches out in mercy and accepts you as a sinner? By birth you have rejected him and his ways and are deserving of death. But instead of abandoning you he enters your world and says in effect, "I love and accept you for who you are, and in spite of your dreadful sin I have died in order to redeem you." What is your initial response to that reality? What does it prompt from you?

_____

_____

_____

_____

Because God loved us even in our sinfulness, he took the initiative by sending Jesus to earth so we all might receive life through him. The good news of the gospel is first a story of God's love, and then a story of God's action.

Read 1 John 4:9-10.

Could you love God if he didn't first love you? Why or why not?

_____

_____

_____

_____

Someone read the following aloud to the group and allow the meaning of these words to penetrate deep into your heart.

> When Adam and Eve made their choice to go their own way, their sin separated them from God. Their sin and the sins of all those born after them left the human race feeling alone and unacceptable.
>
> But how did God feel? Was he judgmental and vindictive? Did he never again want anything to do with the human creation that had rebelled against him?
>
> Instead of anger, God felt grief and sadness. One generation after another, his cherished humans lived a life of sin and rebellion, and "it broke his heart" (Genesis 6:6).
>
> Imagine God as he watches in grief and sadness while your own generation commits sin after sin and suffers the consequences of those sins. He was there when you were born into the very world where he and the first human couple had once walked in perfect relationship. God must have watched with sadness because you and I were born into a world where he was once able to live in perfect relationship with humanity. But because of sin, you were separated from him—dead to him and unable to relate to him—all because of your sinful nature.

But instead of rejecting you, he accepts you in spite of your sin. He longs to relate to you and those around you as intimately as he once did to the first humans he created. He wants to take pleasure in you. He wants to see in your eyes the delight that only his life and love can bring. But that's not possible, because your sin separated you from the life that is found in him, even from the moment you were conceived. While his heart accepts you without condition, his holiness cannot embrace your life of selfishness. For you have followed in Adam and Eve's footsteps, becoming his enemy by repeatedly and selfishly choosing your own sinful ways instead of his holy ways.

You are the one who desperately needs him, but you haven't sought him out. You are the one who should have been crying out for help. You have rejected him, but he still accepted you. The all-sufficient Lord, who "has no needs…[but] gives life and breath to everything, and…satisfies every need there is" *wants you* (Acts 17:25). He wants to relate to you—to enjoy and delight and take pleasure in a personal relationship with you. He wants to complete your joy. So what did God do? He took the initiative.

God entered your world in human form in order to cancel the curse of sin and death that has power over you. He performed the miracle of the incarnation, whereby he "became human and lived here on earth among us" (John 1:14). "Because God's children are human beings—made of flesh and blood—Jesus also became flesh and blood by being born in human form. For only as a human being could he die, and only by dying could he break the power of the Devil, who had the power of death" (Hebrews 2:14).

Through the incarnation God says, "You may have turned away from me, but I'm not turning away from you. I accept you without condition. You are so important to me that I will go to extraordinary lengths to form a personal relationship with you. I'll enter your world and become human like you to save you from death and eternal aloneness without me."

Truth Encounter

Someone read John 1:14 and Romans 8:15-16.

Now, in the quiet of this moment, let your heart express to God your gratefulness for his love and mercy to you. Thank him for becoming flesh—for entering this world to redeem you. Praise him for his unfailing love toward you. Tell him of your gratitude for how you have been given the right to become his child. Take time to write out your words of thanksgiving.

_____

_____

_____

_____

_____

_____

_____

Share your heart of gratitude with other group members. Praise God together. Sing a song of thanksgiving. Someone read Psalm 63:1-8, and everyone continue your thanks to God for the incarnation.

Then in unison read your faith statement.

> **We believe the truth of the incarnation (God becoming human), in which God accepted us without condition and sent Jesus Christ, born of the Virgin Mary, to redeem us and restore us to a relationship with him.**

Consider singing a song of worship. Pray together thanking God for his love and mercy.

TruthTalk—An Assignment of the Week

This week share with a family member or friend how grateful you are for the incarnation. Consider saying something like:

1 "From this week's small group I have a new gratitude for God's plan to send Jesus to earth. From the very beginning, God was moved to action because of his desire for a relationship with me! That's meaningful to me because…

_____

_____

_____

_____

_____."

God…took the initiative. We are the ones who desperately need him, but we didn't seek him out…Yet the all-sufficient Lord, who "has no needs… [but] gives life and breath to everything, and…satisfies every need there is" *wants you and wants me* **(Acts 17:25). We rejected him yet he still accepted us. He wants to relate to us—to enjoy and delight and take pleasure in a personal relationship with us. He wants to complete our joy.**

2 "The story of Christ's birth and how he came to earth means more to me this year because…

_____

_____

_____

_____

_____."

3 "As a parent, I was reflecting on how much I love you and then how amazed I am that God gave up his only Son so we could relate to him. That kind of love is incredible to me because…

_____

_____

_____

_____

_____."

Read chapter 17 of *The Unshakable Truth* book.

Evidence that God Became Human in the Form of Jesus

Review: How did your TruthTalk assignment go this week? What was the response?

_____

_____

_____

_____

As a small child, what did you believe Santa Claus did on Christmas Eve? When did you stop believing in him, and why?

_____

_____

_____

_____

At some point children figure out that Santa Claus is a myth—a fantasy character that encourages giving at Christmastime. But there is no real evidence that such a person with such magical powers ever existed. But how about Jesus as the Son of God—is there evidence he was who he claimed to be?

Some say Jesus is the Creator God who took on human form to save us. Is that true, or is Jesus also a myth? Does it really matter if he actually was God's Son in human form? Or, is the point just to believe he was God? Why or why not?

_____

_____

_____

_____

_____

_____

OUR GROUP OBJECTIVE

To gain a greater confidence in the truth that Jesus was God in human form, who came to redeem us and lets us know he truly understands us.

Someone read the following. (This is drawn from chapter 17 of *The Unshakable Truth* book.)

> We celebrate the birth of Jesus Christ year after year. We proclaim the miraculous incarnation— God taking on human form. We preach about a God full of love and acceptance, who entered our world to save us from eternal death. And though the Scripture says God "became human and lived here on earth among us" (John 1:14), how can we really know if he actually showed up to demonstrate his acceptance and love for us?
>
> That question may sound cynical, but the reality is, God himself wants to assure us that he actually came to earth to redeem us. That is why he had an angel declare to shepherds, "I bring you good news of great joy for everyone! The Savior— yes, the Messiah, the Lord—has been born tonight in Bethlehem, the city of David!" (Luke 2:10-11). He wanted to assure those living at the time that Mary's baby was actually the Son of God—the Supreme Being coming to redeem them. God wants us to believe with confidence that his Son, born 2000 years ago, is our redeemer as well. But in today's world some people doubt Jesus was who he claimed to be. Even you may harbor some doubts. Is it wrong to have a few doubts or questions about such an important issue?

Do you think Jesus was offended by his disciple Thomas when he said, "I won't believe it [that Jesus rose from the dead] unless I see the nail wounds in his hands, put my fingers into them, and place my hand into the wound in his side" (John 20:25)? Why or why not?

_____

_____

_____

_____

Someone read John 20:27-31.

In part, why did Christ's followers document his many miraculous signs?

_____

_____

_____

_____

Someone read the following.

> God's Word was given to us, in part, to provide us with convincing evidence that Jesus was who he claimed to be and our redeemer. God is not troubled by our questions. He wants us to have answers and he has given us sufficient evidence to answer our questions.
>
> There are at least three things that tell us that Jesus was God in the flesh. Those things are his miracles,

Messianic prophecy, and his virgin birth. We will focus in this session on his virgin birth. The other two areas will be covered in other Unshakable Truth Journey growth guides.

Before we look at Jesus' being born of a virgin, which would confirm his deity, let's examine what he claimed. Why? Because some today say that it is individual Christians and the church who make Jesus out to be God. The assertion is that he never claimed to be God—he only said he was the Son of Man, which implies he wasn't making a claim to deity.

Someone read John 14:6.

What was Jesus claiming here?

_____

_____

_____

_____

This passage shows that Jesus had no question about who he was.

Someone read John 17:1-3.

Who was Jesus saying he was, who his Father was, and who sent him to earth? Who gives eternal life?

_____

_____

_____

_____

Is there any question that Jesus knew who he was and declared it plainly to others?

Someone read Mark 14:61-64.

What did Jesus claim that caused the Jewish high priest and the Jewish religious council (the Sanhedrin) to condemn him to death?

_____

_____

_____

_____

The Jewish high council understood clearly what Jesus was claiming and called for the death sentence because of his claim.

Born of a Virgin

A clear sign that Jesus was God in human form is his virgin birth.

Someone read Isaiah 7:14 and Matthew 1:20-24. (The Matthew passage quotes from Isaiah 7.)

What did the prophet Isaiah prophesy 700 years before Jesus was born?

_____

_____

Why do you think it took an angel coming to Joseph in a dream to convince him of this prophecy?

_____

_____

_____

Someone read the following.

> What striking words: "The virgin will be with child" or "The *virgin* will *conceive*." In the course of nature, virgins don't conceive. Conception requires fertilization of the female's ovum (egg) by the male's gamete (sperm) to form a new cell, called a zygote. The zygote must then implant itself in the lining of the uterus. That single cell possesses a complete set of chromosomes containing genetic information, half of which comes from the father and half from the mother.
>
> But God, speaking through the prophet Isaiah, promised something that human history had never seen before (nor has it since): A child would be born outside the natural process of conception. Instead, the Holy Spirit of God himself would form,

in the dark ocean of a virgin's womb, a child of divine origin. This person would bear a unique identity because the infinite God would be his father and a finite human virgin would be his mother—thus the God-man would be born. From that miraculous moment of conception, that God-human fetus would develop from a single cell into sixty trillion cells and would be brought into the world as "Immanuel—'God is with us'" (Isaiah 7:14).

If Jesus was virgin-born then Joseph wasn't his birth father. And in that case people who knew Jesus' family would—apart from a miraculous virgin birth—naturally conclude Jesus was born out of wedlock. So was this the case?

Note that certain Jewish leaders were arguing with Jesus that their father was Abraham. Someone read John 8:39-41.

What were the leaders' slanderous remarks about Jesus' birth?

_____

_____

_____

_____

In Jesus' day children were called by the name of their fathers—except, of course, in the case of children whose paternity was doubted. What did Jesus' hometown people call him? Someone read Mark 6:1-3.

_____

_____

Someone read the following.

> Think about it. Joseph would have been the hardest man on the planet to convince of Mary's story that she was a virgin. He was the man most closely affected. He was the man who would, for the rest of his life, be ridiculed for marrying an unfaithful, pregnant woman who was bearing another man's child. He would have to endure the contempt of the men in the town, who would forever look on him as too stupid not to believe Mary's wild story about God making her pregnant. He would have to endure the humiliation of being married to a shamed woman and raising, as would be said, the child of her adultery.
>
> Yet it's clear that Joseph was not stupid and made his decision fully aware of its implications. The fact that he did not believe Mary at first and resolved to break the engagement, just as any man would, shows us he was not stupid. It shows us he knew full well the implications of violating social expectations about purity and the sanctity of marriage.

A good and prudent man, as Matthew calls him, would be well aware of how marrying Mary would mar his reputation for the rest of his life. So why would he go on and marry the girl? Only one reason makes any sense at all. He knew the truth. He actually received a message from an angel, and that message delivered to him was the absolute truth. Mary was a virgin who was bearing in her womb the Son of God.

The evidence for the virgin birth not only points to the conclusion that Jesus of Nazareth is who he claimed to be, the Son of the living God; it also shows how much he identified with us. Though he was God, he humbled himself and willingly endured the sneers and scorn of those who didn't believe in him. The evidence of Christ's deity through the miracle of the virgin birth is just one of the truths God has given us to reinforce that he accepted us in spite of our sin and sent the one and only person who could redeem us.

Truth Encounter

Someone read Philippians 3:10.

God is God, and he knows you for who you are and what you have gone through. Yet does it somehow mean more to you that he suffered as a human like you have suffered? Why or why not?

_____

_____

_____

_____

Someone read the following.

> With the miracle of the virgin birth and the well-known beauty of the Christmas story, we may often miss the controversy that Jesus endured. We may forget the lifelong rejection and shame he suffered.
>
> The writer of Hebrews tells us that Christ "has gone through suffering and temptation…[and] is able to help us when we are being tempted…[He] understands our weaknesses, for he faced all of the same temptations we do, yet he did not sin. So let us come boldly…and we will find grace to help us when we need it" (Hebrews 2:18; 4:15-16). There is nothing you have experienced that God in Christ does not understand firsthand! He, like you, has experienced…

- rejection—by his own people
- abandonment—by his own disciples
- misunderstanding—by his own followers
- ridicule—at his own trial
- betrayal—by a close friend
- criticism—by the religious leaders of his day

He has experienced all the ups—and downs—of human existence. He's "been there, done that"—wherever you have been.

Can you relate to some of the painful moments of Jesus' life? Identify some of your own painful experiences from the above list that Jesus endured.

_____

_____

_____

_____

Now take the next few moments and quietly reflect on the sufferings of our Savior. Christ experienced the painful rejection of those closest to him. He was abandoned, misunderstood, ridiculed, criticized, and betrayed.

What do you feel for Jesus as you consider all that he endured? Can you tell him how sad it makes you feel to know of his sufferings? Complete this sentence:

"Jesus, I feel such sadness/sorrow/compassion when I imagine how you endured…

_____
_____
_____
_____."

Share with your group what you wrote and how you feel for Jesus.

Complete this sentence and share your answer with your group.

"Jesus, I also feel such gratitude/humility/thankfulness that you are a Savior who…

_____
_____
_____
_____."

Pray together with one or two others in your group. Enjoy the privilege of sharing in the fellowship of Christ's sufferings. Consider singing songs of worship.

TruthTalk—An Assignment of the Week

This week share with a member of your family or a friend what you have discovered in this session. Consider saying something like:

All that Jesus said and did pointed to his identity as the Deity and the Messiah, and all of it pointed to the purpose for which he came to earth. If he is not who he claimed to be, then his teachings are either the rantings of a lunatic who sincerely *thought* he was God (but wasn't) or the words of a liar who *knew* he wasn't God (but said he was).

1 "In our group this week we were studying how Jesus was God in human form. Let me tell you what I've learned about the miracle of Jesus being born of a virgin:

_____

_____

_____

_____."

2 "I have a new appreciation and admiration for the Christmas story. After the beautiful story in the manger, Jesus' life was filled with controversy. That's been meaningful to me because…

_____

_____

_____

_____."

3 "The Christmas story is wonderful because it's the story of Jesus' birth. God did amazing miracles when he sent his Son to earth. This story also helps us remember that as Jesus grew up, there were some people who made fun of him. The people didn't believe that God was Jesus' father, and because of that he endured ridicule, misunderstanding, rejection, and abandonment and eventually died a cruel death for us. When I think of what he went through, I feel…

_____

_____

_____

_____."

Read chapter 18 of *The Unshakable Truth* book. Also note pages 181–183. These pages give practical examples to share during the holiday season.

HOW WE ARE UNCONDITIONALLY LOVED AND ACCEPTED

Review: How did your TruthTalk assignment go this week? What was the response?

_____

_____

_____

_____

What causes people to thank you and give you praise? Think of situations that bring you praise at work, with friends playing sports, and at home with family. Complete the following sentences.

I get praised or thanked at work when I _____

_____.

I get praised or thanked when playing a game with friends when I _____.

I get praised or thanked at home when I _____

_____.

What does praise for a job well done tell you about your worth as a person? Does acceptable behavior define your worth as a person? Why or why not?

_____

_____

_____

_____

Be honest—do most people tend to value you on the basis of what you do or can do for them? Why or why not?

_____

_____

_____

_____

OUR GROUP OBJECTIVE

To discover the deeper meaning of God's unconditional acceptance and what it means to each of us.

Someone read Romans 5:8 and 1 Peter 1:18-19.

As a sinner your behavior is completely unacceptable. So how much does God consider you are worth as a sinner? How much did God pay to ransom you?

_____

_____

_____

_____

Someone read the following.

How can God accept us without condition when we are sinners and his enemy? How can he say we are worth the high price of Jesus when our behavior is so unacceptable? What many in our culture today believe is that a person's behavior and lifestyle represents *who they are*. If that viewpoint was written equation-style it would look like this:

Who I Am = What I Do

Who I Am = What I Have

With this thinking, who you are is inseparable from what you do and have and think and believe. That means your identity and worth are wrapped up in your conduct and possessions. What you do and have therefore represents who you are. What you do and have in life therefore determines how much you are worth. But is this how God views us—our actions and possessions as inseparable with our person?

Someone read Psalm 103:8-12 and Micah 7:18-19.

If our behavior were inseparable from our person, could God do what these passages say he does with our sin? What does this tell us about the way he views who we are and what we do? Discuss.

_____

_____

_____

_____

It is clear God doesn't excuse our sin. Yet he is able to see our sin separately from who he created us to be—a person of great worth created in his image and likeness. His unconditional acceptance of you is not performance-based. So if his acceptance isn't based on your performance, what is it based on? Read 1 John 4:9-10 and write your thoughts here.

_____

_____

_____

_____

_____

_____

How Jesus' Love Defines Our Worth

Someone read John 4:7-9.

As far as the Jews were concerned, Samaritans were the lowest of the low—not even worthy of conversing with. In this incident, why would Jesus be motivated to even talk with this Samaritan woman?

_____

_____

_____

_____

Now read John 4:10-14.

Why is Jesus wanting to give this outcast woman living water? Again, what is his motivation? The key is in Jesus' prayer to his Father found in the book of John. Someone read John 17:9-10. Put your thoughts here.

_____

_____

_____

_____

_____

_____

Someone read the following:

Although Jesus exposed the Samaritan woman's sin, he engaged her in conversation without judgment or condemnation. Her adulterous behavior was unacceptable to him, yet he looked beyond her faults and saw her need for a relationship. This woman was alienated and alone. As a sinner and a daughter of Eve she was separated from God. But Jesus knew this lost child belonged to his Father, and she belonged to him too. For she was his glory, his masterpiece, his shining trophy, and he wanted her back.

It is true the Samaritan woman was tarnished by sin. As a trophy she was far from shining when Jesus wanted her to be his closest friend. He wants you too. It is his desire for a relationship with you that makes you the most valuable possession in the universe. The fact that Jesus is passionate about relating to you personally defines your very worth. The Holy and Almighty God, who is perfect in all his ways and in need of nothing, says: "I want you personally as my friend. And you are so valuable to me that I will go to extraordinary lengths to secure your eternal friendship."

The Incarnate One does not condemn you or criticize you, even though your behavior may be unacceptable. He doesn't condone or overlook your sin either; it must be dealt with on his terms. But he

loves you for who you are—the unique, one-of-a-
kind individual he created. And he accepts you at
the point of your failure. See yourself in light of his
grace and embrace his love. Resist the temptation
to engage in self-condemnation, because accepting
your unconditional acceptance will result in the joy
of a safe and secure relationship.

Truth Encounter

Do you tend to struggle with self-condemnation and a sense
of low worth at times? Do you sometimes allow others and the
things of this world to define your value? What about allowing
Jesus' love to define your worth? Discuss.

_____

_____

_____

_____

_____

_____

_____

Jesus would like to speak to you through the Holy Spirit and
let you know how his acceptance of you brings you the joy

of security in him. As a time of worship to him, someone read Romans 8:31-39 slowly.

Allow the truth of these words to penetrate deeply into your heart—he loves you—he wants you—he will never leave you. Pause from time to time as the verses are read and share with others in the group what Jesus is saying to you.

_____

_____

_____

_____

_____

_____

Rejoice in the experience of a love that will not die. Consider singing a song together. Pray together and give thanks to a God who accepts us without condition.

_____

_____

_____

_____

_____

_____

_____

TruthTalk—An Assignment of the Week

This week share with a family member or friend what it feels like to be accepted for who you are. Consider saying something like:

Jesus not only accepts us for who we are, he identifies with all that we feel. He knows what we are going through, no matter what it is, and he understands it like no other. And that creates a bond and intimacy like nothing else can… By becoming a human being, he let us know how intimately and completely he identifies with us—and with all we experience.

1 "This week in group I had a new experience of the way God sees me. It is liberating to know and sense that he…

_____
_____
_____
_____."

2 "I have a new perspective on how God sees me. I now know that he sees me with eyes of grace—for who I am, not just for what I do. I'd like to tell you what a difference that's made for me. It has…

_____
_____
_____
_____."

3 "I've been learning how God sees me for who I am—apart from what I do. I would like to grow more in my ability to do that with you too. So I've been noticing some of the great character traits you have. I've been especially impressed by your…

_____

_____

_____

_____."

Read chapter 19 of *The Unshakable Truth* book.

ACCEPTING OTHERS AS CHRIST ACCEPTS US

Review: How did your TruthTalk assignment go this week? What was the response?

_____

_____

_____

_____

Think of a time when you were a child and you really messed up—you did something that was clearly wrong and you were disciplined for it. What did you do and how did your parent(s) respond to you? Did you feel very accepted at the moment? Why or why not?

_____

_____

_____

_____

OUR GROUP OBJECTIVE

To gain a deeper understanding of what it takes to accept others as Christ accepts us and to practice what that sounds and looks like.

How do we respond to our own children or friends when they mess up? How do you balance addressing a person's misbehavior with not making him or her feel rejected as a person?

_____

_____

_____

_____

_____

Someone read Romans 15:7.

How does Christ respond to us when we mess up? How does he address our behavior without making us feel rejected as a person?

_____

_____

_____

_____

_____

What is the difference between acceptance of a person and approval of their behavior? Do we sometimes get these two confused?

- *Acceptance:* Deliberate and ready reception; receiving willingly; focuses more on the value of the person for who they are.

- *Approval:* Affirming as satisfactory; expressing a favorable opinion; focuses more on what a person does than what is being accomplished.

Discuss what happens when we express disapproval of a person's behavior before they feel accepted for who they are.

_____

_____

_____

_____

_____

_____

_____

|||||||||||||||||||||||||||||||||||||||||||||||||||||||||||||||||||||||||||||||||||||||||

The Acceptance of the Father

Someone read the following.

> The story of the prodigal son tells us of a young man who demanded his inheritance from his father,

left home, and squandered it all. He ended up feed-
ing pigs. So he decided to go back home and ask his
father if he could become a servant (a hired hand).

Someone read Luke 15:20.

Did the son have to go looking for his dad when he got home?
What is the significance of how the father responded?

_____

_____

_____

_____

What was the attitude of the son? Did he make excuses for his
behavior, try to cut a deal with his dad, or what?

_____

_____

_____

_____

Someone read Luke 15:22-24.

What was the father's response to the idea that the son no
longer be called "son" but take on the role of a servant? What is
the significance of the father's response?

_____

_____

_____

_____

Someone read the following.

It's natural for the prodigal to no longer feel worthy because of his rebellious behavior. In some respects he thought he could at least barter his room and board through working as a servant. But the man separated the boy's behavior from who he really was. He accepted him on the basis of his long-standing relationship—he was his son. Because of the father-son relationship the man looked beyond his boy's faults and saw his need for a continuing relationship with a dad.

Christlike acceptance is able to separate us as a person from our behavior. Wrong behavior must be addressed, but not at the expense of making us feeling rejected for who we are. When we don't feel accepted for who we are, faults and all, we can easily feel personally rejected when our performance is questioned.

What happens when a child doesn't feel accepted for who he or she is? Say your daughter comes home with her report card. She has gotten two D's. You sit her down and explain that those grades are unacceptable. You tell her she can't have any more sleepovers until her grades come up.

How have your children responded to your disapproval and correction? Have they felt emotionally accepted yet realized

their actions were wrong? Or have they felt emotionally rejected? Do you sense that the cultural thinking *Who I Am = What I Do or What I Have* is playing a role here?

_____

_____

_____

_____

Let's say your daughter feels you understand her clearly for who she is. She knows you see all her strengths and weaknesses, her qualities and faults, and you have conveyed over and over you still love what you see. What happens when you identify a behavior that needs to be corrected? She doesn't feel indicted as a person, she feels accepted as a daughter. Yet if she doesn't feel accepted and understood first and foremost, she will feel any questioning of her performance as a rejection of her as a person, which is how many young people feel today.

Approval and acceptance are to live in delicate balance with each other. Acceptance is the foundation upon which approval is to be built. Give healthy doses of approval without the foundation of acceptance, and a performance-based relationship is formed. Give acceptance without ever addressing performance and a permissive relationship is formed. However, if we convince children we love and accept them for who they are, we can then address their behavior without their feeling rejected as a person.

But even in giving approval we should focus more on the person's value in accomplishing a task. Healthy approval doesn't highlight *what* has been accomplished as much as *why* it was accomplished. When we place the value on a person's character qualities and gifts that enable success—qualities such as determination, persistence, creativity, faithfulness, and so on, we are able to keep the focus on the worth of the person.

When God the Father gave his approval of his Son, Jesus, he said for all to hear, "You are my Son, whom I love; with you I am well pleased" (Mark 1:11 NIV). God placed his "well pleased" approval within the context of the father-son relationship and the relational love he had for his Son. Jesus communicated this truth when he told of the master's approval of his servant: "The master was full of praise. 'Well done, my good and faithful servant'" (Matthew 25:21). Again, "well done" was placed within the context of a focus on the goodness of the servant and the faithfulness of the servant. The more we can focus our approval on the qualities and gifts of the person, the more we will avoid performance-based relationships.

"Accept each other just as Christ has accepted you; then God will be glorified" (Romans 15:7). It is Jesus' type of acceptance we all desire. As we receive it from him we feel safe and secure. And when we accept others in that way, they too feel safe and secure. That is the kind of relationship that brings us joy and God glory.

Truth Encounter

Someone read Romans 15:7.

We all have the need for acceptance. So what might the *need* for acceptance sound like?

To help you get started, complete these sentences.

"Please allow me to make mistakes, but still _____
_____."

"I know I'm not perfect, but I need you to look beyond _____
_____."

Other expressions of the need for acceptance might be…

_____
_____

_____

_____

_____

_____

What might heartfelt acceptance sound like?

To get you started, complete these sentences.

> Your 17-year-old son calls you rather late in the evening and
> says, "I just had an accident with your car." You say " Tell me
>
> _____
>
> _____
>
> _____."

> Your husband went to the store to pick up various last-
> minute items for your important dinner plans for a special
> guest. You want the evening to be just perfect. As everyone
> is about to sit down to eat you find that your husband failed
> to get a critical item on the list. You glare at him. He pulls
> you off to the side and says, "I just forgot to write that item
> down—I'm sorry." You say, " I realize you forgot it
>
> _____
>
> _____
>
> _____."

Think of a fault or weakness you have that sometimes incon-
veniences or even irritates your spouse or friends. When you

exhibit this weakness in a situation, what would you like to hear said to you? Describe a situation and what you long to hear.

_____

_____

_____

_____

What might genuine acceptance look like?

You just had a disagreement or clash of wills with your son, daughter, spouse, or friend. What form of action would genuine acceptance take—what might it look like?

_____

_____

_____

_____

_____

_____

Now break into smaller groups, or just go around the room, and express Christlike acceptance to one another. You can begin with someone sharing how he or she may have disappointed someone else in the room at some point; didn't follow through with a task; or simply didn't live up to another's expectation. At that point one or more of you express heartfelt words of acceptance to that person.

Note: This exercise might also be a good time to have spouses pair off and experience renewed acceptance of each other.

Then pause to ask God, "How could I better express acceptance of others?" Listen—be still. Allow God's Spirit to reveal who needs to receive his grace of acceptance through you. Then complete the following sentences:

"I could better express God's acceptance to _____ *(name)* by allowing God to live through me and doing _____

_____

_____

_____

_____

_____."

Share the above with your group to indicate how God would be pleased to minister some of his acceptance through you to someone specific this week.

Truth Talk—An Assignment of the Week

This week share with a family member or friend Godlike acceptance. Consider saying something like:

1 "I am so grateful for God's acceptance of me. He doesn't love me

If we are to live out Godlike acceptance in our own lives, we must learn to accept others for who they are, no matter what. Then God will be glorified, and others will experience a relational connection that reflects Christ's connection to us. And that kind of connection will foster the joy of secure relationships and will help us to pass on our faith to others.

when I shape up or when I get my life together. He just loves me for who I am. And that truth is so meaningful to me because…

_____

_____

_____

_____."

2 "I have realized I need to be more accepting of others. I was recently impressed with how God accepts me and doesn't expect me to change before he extends his love. I need to be more like Jesus in this way because…

_____

_____

_____

_____."

3 "I know _____ has been hard for you lately. I want you to know that I am here for you and want to offer my support and acceptance. God has shown me that

he loves me without trying to 'fix'
me. I will stop trying to 'fix' you
and the situation. I just want to be
more accepting of you by…

_____

_____

_____

_____."

This week review chapters 16 through 19 of *The Unshakable Truth* book.

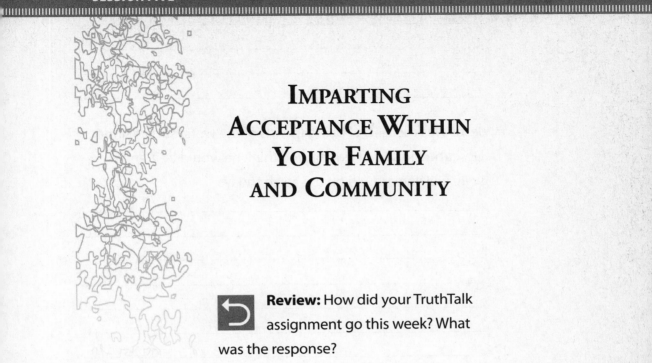

IMPARTING ACCEPTANCE WITHIN YOUR FAMILY AND COMMUNITY

Review: How did your TruthTalk assignment go this week? What was the response?

_____

_____

_____

_____

Someone read Luke 5:17-30; 7:39; and 15:1.

Why do you think the religious leaders found it so offensive that Jesus talked with, ate with, and associated with the despicable, the outcasts, and the sinners of the community?

_____

_____

_____

_____

_____

_____

_____

Jesus was accused of being friends of the worst sort of sinners. Describe the sort of sinners you think he would befriend if he were walking around on the earth today.

_____

_____

_____

_____

_____

_____

_____

Someone read the following.

> Remember, accepting others doesn't mean you endorse their behavior or lifestyle. Christlike acceptance means separating a person's actions from the person we are to love. And when we accept those who are considered "unacceptable," "God will be glorified" (Romans 15:7).

OUR GROUP OBJECTIVE

To plan a group activity that involves demonstrating love and care to one or more groups of people considered "unacceptable" to perhaps many others.

In this session you as a group are to brainstorm about an effort to reach out to some people whom others might consider undesirable or unacceptable, or who engage in a lifestyle clearly against scriptural teachings. Your effort should not come across as a means to convince people they are wrong. It should be an expression of the care and love Christ feels for each of them.

Brainstorm: _____

_____

_____

_____

_____

_____

_____

_____

_____

Take the time here to plan your project using the following steps:

Identify your activity: _____
_____
_____
_____

Set the date and time for your activity: _____
_____
_____
_____

Determine what is needed to execute your activity: _____
_____
_____
_____

Assign responsibilities and tasks. Who will be doing what? _____
_____
_____
_____

Have someone in your group track and record what is being done. This is to record the results of your efforts.
_____
_____
_____

Bring every aspect of your activity before the Lord.

Someone read Matthew 5:14-16.

As you close in prayer, ask God that he would be honored and praised as you reflect Christlike acceptance to those around you.

_____

_____

_____

_____

||||||||||||||||||||||||||||||||||||||||||||||||||||||||||||||||||||||||||||||||||||||||||||||||||||||

Assignment of the Week

Execute your activity.

Take the Complete Unshakable Truth® Journey!

The Unshakable Truth Journey gets to the heart of what being a true follower of Christ means and what knowing him is all about. Each five-session course is based one of 12 core truths of the Christian faith presented in Josh and Sean McDowell's book *The Unshakable Truth®*.

The Unshakable Truth Journey is uniquely positioned for today's culture because it 1) highlights how Christianity's beliefs affect relationships, 2) promotes a relational, group context in which Christians can experience the teaching in depth, and 3) shows believers how they can live out Christianity's central truths before their community and world.

More than just a program, The Unshakable Truth Journey is a tool for long-term change and transformation!

CREATED—EXPERIENCE YOUR UNIQUE PURPOSE is devoted to the truth that God is—he exists, and he created human beings for a reason. It lays a foundation for who people are because they're God's creation, who God designed them to be, and how they can live a life of fulfillment.

INSPIRED—EXPERIENCE THE POWER OF GOD'S WORD explores the truth that God has spoken and revealed himself to humanity within the Bible. Further, he gave us his Word for a very clear purpose—to provide for us and protect us.

BROKEN—EXPERIENCE VICTORY OVER SIN examines the truth about humankind's brokenness because of original sin, humankind's ongoing problem with sin, and how instead to make right choices in life.

ACCEPTED—EXPERIENCE GOD'S UNCONDITIONAL LOVE opens up the truth about God's redemption plan. The truth that God became human establishes his unconditional acceptance of us, which defines our worth. God values us in spite of our sin. This is the basis on which we gain a high sense of worth.

SACRIFICE—EXPERIENCE A DEEPER WAY TO LOVE digs into the truth about Christ's atonement. The truth that Christ had to die to purchase our salvation shows the true meaning of love—and how God can bring us into a right relationship with him in spite of our sin.

FORGIVEN—EXPERIENCE THE SURPRISING GRACE OF GOD explores the truth about the power of God's grace. The truth that God can offer us forgiveness in spite of our sin helps us understand how we actually obtain a relationship with him.

GROWING—EXPERIENCE THE DYNAMIC PATH TO TRANSFORMATION speaks to the truth about our transformed life in Christ. The truth about our transformed life in Christ defines who we are in this world and shows how we can know our purpose in life.

RESURRECTED—EXPERIENCE FREEDOM FROM THE FEAR OF DEATH focuses on the truth about Christ's resurrection. The truth that Christ rose from the grave and that his resurrection is a historical event assures us of eternal life and overcomes any fear of dying.

EMPOWERED—EXPERIENCE LIVING IN THE POWER OF THE SPIRIT covers the truth about the Trinity. The truth that God is three in one and defines how relationships work through the Holy Spirit lays the foundation for how we can experience the power of the Spirit.

PERSPECTIVE—EXPERIENCE THE WORLD THROUGH GOD'S EYES examines the truth about God's kingdom and how it defines a biblical worldview. These sessions show how to gain a biblical worldview.

COMMUNITY—EXPERIENCE JESUS ALIVE IN HIS PEOPLE opens up the truth about the church. The truth about Christ's body—the church—provides us with our mission in life and shows us how to experience true community.

RESTORED—EXPERIENCE THE JOY OF YOUR DESTINY is devoted to the truth about the return of Christ. The truth that Jesus is coming back helps us grasp our destiny in life and gain an eternal perspective on life and death.

The Unshakable Truth Journey
Accepted Growth Guide Evaluation Form

1. How many on average participated in your group? _____

2. Did you read all or a portion of *The Unshakable Truth* book? _____

3. Did your group leader use visual illustrations during this course? _____

4. *Group leader:* Was your experience connecting to the web and viewing the video illustrations acceptable? Explain.

   _____

   _____

5. On a scale of 1 to 10 (10 being the highest) how would you rate:
   a) the quality and usefulness of the session content? _____
   b) the responsiveness and interaction of those in your group? _____

6. To what degree did this course deepen your practical understanding of the truths it covered?
   ❏ Little   ❏ Somewhat   ❏ Rather considerably

   Please give any comments you feel would be helpful to us.

   _____

   _____

   _____

   _____

Please mail to: Josh McDowell Evaluation
                 PO Box 4126
                 Copley, OH 44321

OTHER HARVEST HOUSE BOOKS BY JOSH McDOWELL AND SEAN McDOWELL

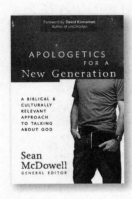

Apologetics for a New Generation
A Biblical and Culturally Relevant Approach to Talking About God
Sean McDowell

This generation's faith is constantly under attack from the secular media, skeptical teachers, and unbelieving peers. You may wonder, *How can I help?*

Working with young adults every day, Sean McDowell understands their situation and shares your concern. His first-rate team of contributors shows how you can help members of the new generation plant their feet firmly on the truth. Find out how you can walk them through the process of...

- formulating a biblical worldview and applying scriptural principles to everyday issues

- articulating their questions and addressing their doubts in a safe environment

- becoming confident in their faith and effective in their witness

The truth never gets old, but people need to hear it in fresh, new ways. Find out how you can effectively share the answers to life's big questions with a new generation.

The Awesome Book of Bible Answers for Kids
Josh McDowell and Kevin Johnson

These concise, welcoming answers include key Bible verses and explorations of topics that matter most to kids ages 8 to 12: God's love; right and wrong; Jesus, the Holy Spirit, and God's Word; different beliefs and religions; church, prayer, and sharing faith. Josh and Kevin look at questions like…

- How do I know God wants to be my friend?

- Are parts of the Bible make-believe, or is everything true?

- Was Jesus a wimp?

- Why do some Christians not act like Christians?

- Can God make bad things turn out okay?

The next time a child in your life asks a good question, this practical and engaging volume will give you helpful tips and conversation ideas so you can connect with them and offer straight talk about faith in Jesus. *Includes an easy-to-use learning and conversation guide.*

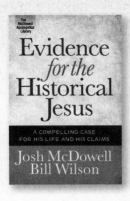

Evidence for the Historical Jesus
A Compelling Case for His Life and His Claims
Josh McDowell and Bill Wilson

After two years of intensive research, the agnostic Josh McDowell was convinced of the reliability of the historical evidence showing that Jesus of Nazareth existed and was precisely who He said He was—God in the flesh. Confronted by the living Lord, Josh accepted the offer of a relationship with Him.

In *Evidence for the Historical Jesus,* Josh teams with writer-researcher Bill Wilson to provide you with a thorough analysis to document that Jesus Christ actually walked on this earth—and that the New Testament accounts are incredibly reliable in describing His life. The authors' broad-ranging investigation examines

- the writings of ancient rabbis, martyrs, and early church leaders

- the evidence of the New Testament text

- historical geography and archaeology

Detailed and incisive but accessible, this volume will help you relate to people who distort or discount Christianity and its Founder. And it will strengthen your confidence in Jesus Christ and in the Scriptures that document His words, His life, and His love.

Why aren't parents the primary disciplers of their children?

Is it even possible to reach today's students and young adults?

Confronting the Fear of Losing Our Kids

Will the majority of our kids continue to walk away from the church and never return?

Involve your church, small group or family in

The Unshakable TRUTH® *Journey*

To expand the impact of the twelve Unshakable Truth® Journey Growth Guides, a complete collection of teaching outlines, leaders' materials, video clips and powerpoints are available for church, small group and family use. For more information visit:

www.UnshakableTruth.com

"How did the early church effectively pass on their faith to every generation for five generations? We owe it to ourselves and our young people to find out."

Josh McDowell

The Unshakable Truth® church and small group resource collections are part of a unique collaboration between Harvest House Publishers and the Great Commandment Network. The Great Commandment Network is an international network of denominational partners, churches, parachurch ministries and strategic ministry leaders who are committed to the development of ongoing Great Commandment ministries worldwide as they prioritize the powerful simplicity of loving God, loving others and making disciples.

Through accredited trainers, the Great Commandment Network equips churches for ongoing relational ministry utilizing resources from the GC² Experience collection.

The GC² Experience Vision

To provide process-driven resources for a lifelong journey of spiritual formation. Every resource includes intentional opportunities to live out life-changing content within the context of loving God, loving others, and making disciples (Matthew 22:37-40; 28:19-20).

The GC² Experience Process includes:

■ Experiential and transformative content. People are relationally transformed when they encounter Jesus, experience his Word, and engage in authentic community.

■ Opportunities to move through a journey of…

- Exploring Truth in the safety of relationship
- Embracing Truth in a personal way
- Experiencing Truth in everyday life
- Expressing Truth through my identity as a Christ-follower

"Most of us have attended too many meetings and have gone through too many courses, only to conclude: We're leaving unchanged, and the people in our lives can see that we're unchanged. It is time to trust God for something different…a movement of life-changing transformation!"

Dr. David Ferguson
The Great Commandment Network

**The Transforming Promise of
Great Commandment/Great Commission Living**
www.GC2experience.com